STEGOSAURUS

AND OTHER PLATE-BACKED PLANT-EATERS

Prehistoric World
STEGOSAURUS
AND OTHER PLATE-BACKED PLANT-EATERS

VIRGINIA SCHOMP

Benchmark Books

MARSHALL CAVENDISH
NEW YORK

DINOSAURS LIVED MILLIONS OF YEARS AGO. EVERYTHING WE KNOW ABOUT THEM—HOW THEY LOOKED, WALKED, ATE, FOUGHT, MATED, AND RAISED THEIR YOUNG—COMES FROM EDUCATED GUESSES BY THE SCIENTISTS WHO DISCOVER AND STUDY FOSSILS. THE INFORMATION IN THIS BOOK IS BASED ON WHAT MOST SCIENTISTS BELIEVE RIGHT NOW. TOMORROW OR NEXT WEEK OR NEXT YEAR, NEW DISCOVERIES COULD LEAD TO NEW IDEAS. SO KEEP YOUR EYES AND EARS OPEN FOR NEWS FLASHES FROM THE PREHISTORIC WORLD!

Benchmark Books
Marshall Cavendish
99 White Plains Road
Tarrytown, New York 10591-9001
www.marshallcavendish.com

© Marshall Cavendish Corporation 2004

Library of Congress Cataloging-in-Publication Data

Schomp, Virginia.
  Stegosaurus and other plate-backed plant-eaters / Virginia Schomp.
      p. cm. — (Prehistoric world)
Includes bibliographical references and index.
  ISBN 0-7614-1544-0
  1. Stegosaurus—Juvenile literature. 2. Stegosauridae—Juvenile literature. [1. Stegosaurus.
  2. Herbivores, Fossil. 3. Dinosaurs.] I. Title. II. Series: Schomp, Virginia. Prehistoric world.

  QE862.O65S428 2003
  567.915—dc21

                                                        2003001880

Front cover: *Stegosaurus*   Back cover: *Huayangosaurus*   Pages 2–3: *Chialingosaurus*

Photo Credits:

Cover illustration: The Natural History Museum, London / Orbis

The illustrations and photographs in this book are used by permission and through the courtesy of:
Marshall Cavendish Corporation: 2–3, 9, 11, 12–13, 16–17, 18, 20–21, 22, 23, back cover. *The Natural History Museum, London:* John Sibbick, 15; Orbis, 8, 19, 24. *PhotoResearchers, Inc.:* © Francois Gohier, courtesy Western Paleontological Labs, 25.

Map and Dinosaur Family Tree by Robert Romagnoli

Printed in China

1 3 5 6 4 2

For Justin and Samantha Bigness

Contents

PRICKLY PLANT-EATERS

A *Stegosaurus* plods toward a water hole. Dipping its head, the dinosaur takes a long, cooling drink. A sudden noise signals danger. It is a fierce *Allosaurus!* With a roar, the hungry hunter bares its daggerlike teeth. But the *Stegosaurus* does not run. Instead it turns its back and swings its tail. At the tip of that tail are four long, sharp spikes. Now the *Stegosaurus* does not look quite so appetizing—and the *Allosaurus* stomps off to find an easier meal.

The long spikes on Stegosaurus's *thick, strong tail protected this peaceful plant-eater from hungry predators.*

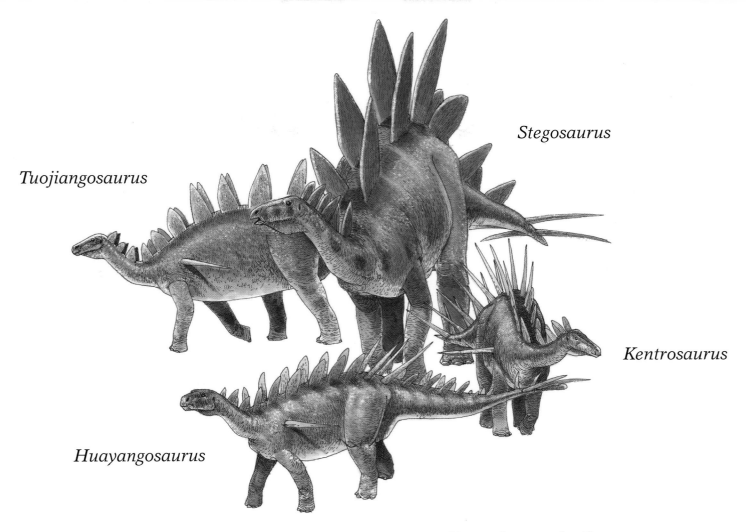

Tuojiangosaurus

Stegosaurus

Kentrosaurus

Huayangosaurus

The stegosaurs all had different arrangements of bony plates and spikes.

Dinosaurs came in many unusual shapes and sizes, and one of the strangest of all was *Stegosaurus*. It belonged to a group of dinosaurs called stegosaurs. The stegosaurs were four-legged plant-eaters. Rows of large bony plates ran along the middle of their backs. Most stegosaurs also had spikes on their tails. On page 26, you can see how *Stegosaurus* and its odd-looking cousins fit into the dinosaur family tree.

One of the smallest stegosaurs was *Huayangosaurus.* About the size of a cow, this peaceful plant-eater had plates and spikes on its back. Medium-sized *Kentrosaurus* was even pricklier. Its double row of narrow, swordlike spikes probably scared off many hungry meat-eaters. But the biggest plate-backed dinosaur—and the one that gave the group its name—was *Stegosaurus.*

The Age of Dinosaurs

Dinosaurs walked the earth during the Mesozoic era, also known as the Age of Dinosaurs. The Mesozoic era lasted from about 250 million to 65 million years ago. It is divided into three periods: the Triassic, Jurassic, and Cretaceous.

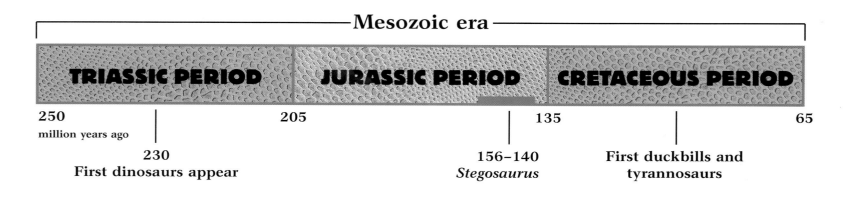

Mesozoic era

TRIASSIC PERIOD   JURASSIC PERIOD   CRETACEOUS PERIOD

250
million years ago

230
First dinosaurs appear

205

156–140
Stegosaurus

135

First duckbills and
tyrannosaurs

65

KENTROSAURUS
(ken-truh-SORE-us)
When: Late Jurassic,
156–150 million years ago
Where: East Africa
- Double row of spikes on back and tail
- One long spike on each side

Kentrosaurus *may have defended itself like a porcupine, stabbing its enemies with its sharp backward-pointing spikes*

A PLATED GIANT

Imagine an animal as big and heavy as two cars. Now give it four sturdy legs and broad feet to carry all that weight. *Stegosaurus*'s hind legs were twice as long as its front legs. That is why its back sloped forward like a slide. Set in two zigzag rows along that humped back were seventeen triangular bony plates. The largest plates, over the dinosaur's hips, were about three times bigger than this page.

At one end of this bulky beast was its muscular tail, tipped with four 3-foot-long spikes. At the other end was a surprisingly small head. *Stegosaurus* had a tiny brain. In fact, its brain was only about the size of a golf ball! But the big plate-backed dinosaur had enough intelligence to survive for millions of years in the dinosaur world.

THE MYSTERY OF THE PLATES

Why did *Stegosaurus* have those puzzling plates? Paleontologists—scientists who study prehistoric life—are not sure. Some believe that the plates were used in self-defense. When a *Stegosaurus* was threatened, blood may have rushed to its plates, turning them an angry red. That made the dinosaur look bigger and scarier. Male stegosaurs also may have used their colorful "blush" to attract mates.

The plates may even have worked as a kind of heating and air-conditioning system. To warm up, the *Stegosaurus* turned to let its plates catch the sun. When the dinosaur was too hot, it turned its plates away from the sun and let the breezes blow through them, cooling its whole body.

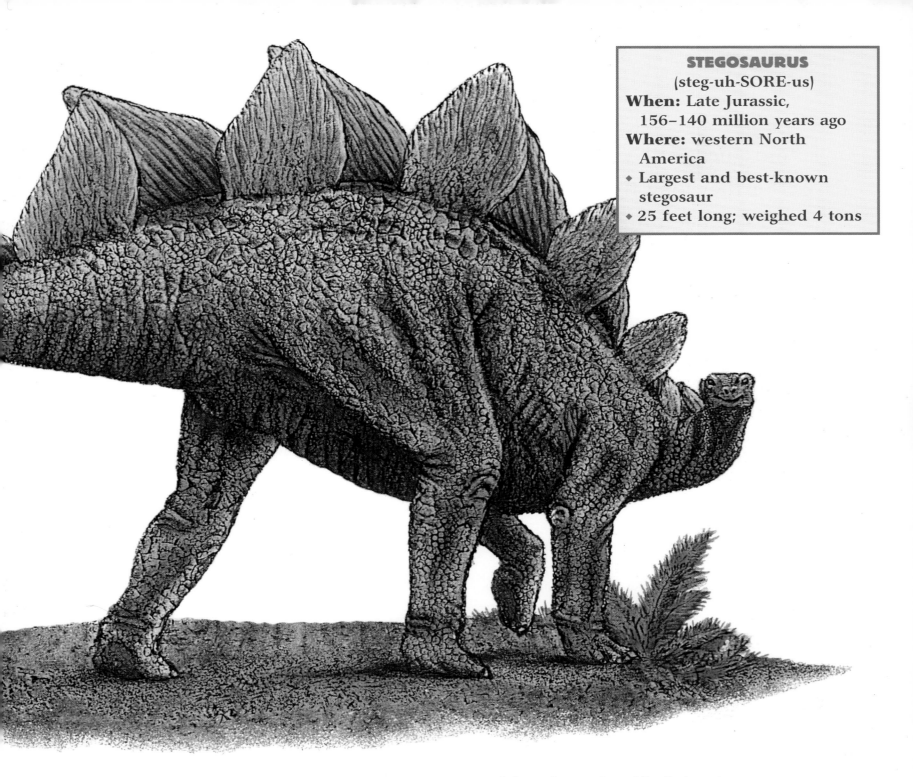

Stegosaurus *was one of the last plate-backed dinosaurs and the only one from North America.*

WHEN DINOSAURS RULED

Dinosaurs walked the earth for about 165 million years. The middle part of that long time span is called the Jurassic period.

At the beginning of the Jurassic period, all the lands on earth were joined together in one giant supercontinent. Slowly that landmass began to break up. The northern part, called Laurasia, drifted away from the southern part, Gondwanaland. Water flowed into the opening, forming a shallow sea.

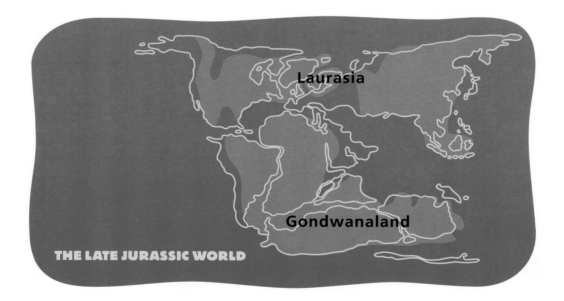

The face of the world is always changing, as the continents slowly move. The yellow outlines on the map show the shape of the modern continents; the green shading shows their position around 140 million years ago, in the days of Stegosaurus.

The ferns, cycads, and other low-growing greens surrounding this Jurassic swamp would make a tasty meal for Stegosaurus.

HOME ON THE PLAINS

Let's take a trip back in time 140 million years, to the Late Jurassic period. The world is warm, wet, and green. Ferns, shrubs, and towering evergreen forests blanket the land.

In western North America, broad plains with many lakes and rivers stretch for hundreds of thousands of miles. One day this area will be known as the Morrison Formation. Now it is the home of *Stegosaurus*.

TUOJIANGOSAURUS
(toh-hwang-oh-SORE-us)
When: Late Jurassic,
156 million years ago
Where: China
◆ Double row of plates from
head to tail
◆ As long as a fire engine

Tuojiangosaurus *had four spikes on its tail for protection from predators.*

Stegosaurus shares its world with many other kinds of dinosaurs. Long-necked *Apatosaurus* feasts on the tops of the tall trees while its shorter cousin *Camarasaurus* gobbles up the lower branches. Deadly *Allosaurus* and *Ceratosaurus* stalk the large plant-eaters. The small but fierce hunter *Ornitholestes* menaces smaller creatures. The dinosaurs rule, but there are other animals, too—flying pterosaurs, long-toothed crocodiles, fish, frogs, lizards, and even small, shy mammals.

A hungry Ceratosaurus *eyes a herd of* Camarasaurus. Ceratosaurus *was just one of the many dangerous predators in the Late Jurassic world.*

LEXOVISAURUS
(lex-oh-vuh-SORE-us)
When: Middle Jurassic,
169–156 million years ago
Where: England and France
◆ Tall, thin plates on neck
and back
◆ Spikes on shoulders and tail

A Lexovisaurus *drinks from a muddy pool. This medium-sized stegosaur was about as long and heavy as a small car.*

PEACEFUL BUT PROTECTED

Stegosaurus had a big stomach to fill. It spent most of its time eating. Lumbering across the plains, with its head close to the ground, the dinosaur searched for ferns, palmlike cycads, and other low-growing plants. Its sharp toothless beak sheared off mouthfuls of tasty greens. The small, weak teeth in the sides of its jaw were not much good for chewing, so the dinosaur probably swallowed most of its meals whole.

Some paleontologists believe that *Stegosaurus* had a trick for reaching the leaves at the top of tall trees. They say that the dinosaur could stand up on its long hind legs. *Stegosaurus*'s strong tail was like the third leg on a tripod, helping to support the dinosaur while it ate.

The small stegosaur Chialingosaurus *fed on low-growing plants and bushes along riverbanks in southern China.*

Dacentrurus *was a small stegosaur with a very spiky tail. It lived and died around the same time as* Stegosaurus.

BATTLE TAILS

Sometimes a hungry predator interrupted *Stegosaurus*'s peaceful feeding. The plate-backed dinosaur was too slow to run away, but it was not defenseless.

Stomping its feet, the stegosaur turned sideways to give its enemy a good look at its tall, red-flushed plates. It swiped its spike-tipped tail. Those long bony spikes could cut deep into a hunter's flesh. Just the sight of that stinging tail was enough to discourage most predators.

Some paleontologists think that *Stegosaurus* lived in herds. Others believe that the big plate-backed dinosaurs were loners, coming together only during the mating season.

HUAYANGOSAURUS
(hwah-yang-uh-SORE-us)
When: Middle Jurassic,
170 million years ago
Where: China
- Earliest known, most primitive stegosaur
- Front and hind legs about the same length

The small horns above this Huayangosaurus's *eyes may indicate that it is a male. Paleontologists have found smaller skeletons without horns, which they think may be the bones of females.*

Wuerhosaurus *was one of the last surviving stegosaurs. It was still living 20 million years after* Stegosaurus *had died out.*

Like all dinosaurs, baby stegosaurs hatched from eggs. Females laid their eggs in nests dug out of the ground. Did they take care of their babies? Or were young *Stegosaurus* left to find food and watch out for predators on their own? Someday paleontologists may find fossils, or hardened remains, of a *Stegosaurus* mother and her babies. Those fossils may help them answer some of the many puzzling questions about the big plate-backed dinosaurs.

These preserved remains of Stegosaurus *were found in the Morrison Formation of western North America. Fossils like this help paleontologists figure out what dinosaurs looked like and how they lived.*

EARLY EXTINCTION

*S*tegosaurus and most of the other plate-backed dinosaurs became extinct—the last of their kind died out—before the end of the Jurassic period. No one knows why. Maybe the stegosaurs could not survive in the world's changing climate. Or maybe they could not compete with new kinds of dinosaurs that appeared, such as the more heavily armored plant-eater *Ankylosaurus.*

Sixty-five million years ago, long after *Stegosaurus* was gone, all the dinosaurs died out. Today paleontologists are still searching, studying, and making exciting new discoveries about life in the Age of Dinosaurs.

Dinosaur Family Tree

ORDER

All dinosaurs are divided into two large groups, based on the shape and position of their hipbones. Ornithischians had backward-pointing hipbones.

SUBORDER

Thyreophorans were four-legged plant-eating dinosaurs with bony plates and armor.

INFRAORDER

Stegosaurs were four-legged plant-eaters with bony plates along their backs.

FAMILY

A family includes one or more types of closely related dinosaurs.

GENUS

Every dinosaur has a two-word name. The first word tells us what genus, or type, of dinosaur it is. The genus plus the second word are its species—the group of very similar animals it belongs to. (For example, *Stegosaurus armatus* is one species of *Stegosaurus*.)

Scientists organize all living things into groups, according to features shared.
This chart shows the groupings of the plate-backed plant-eaters described in this book.

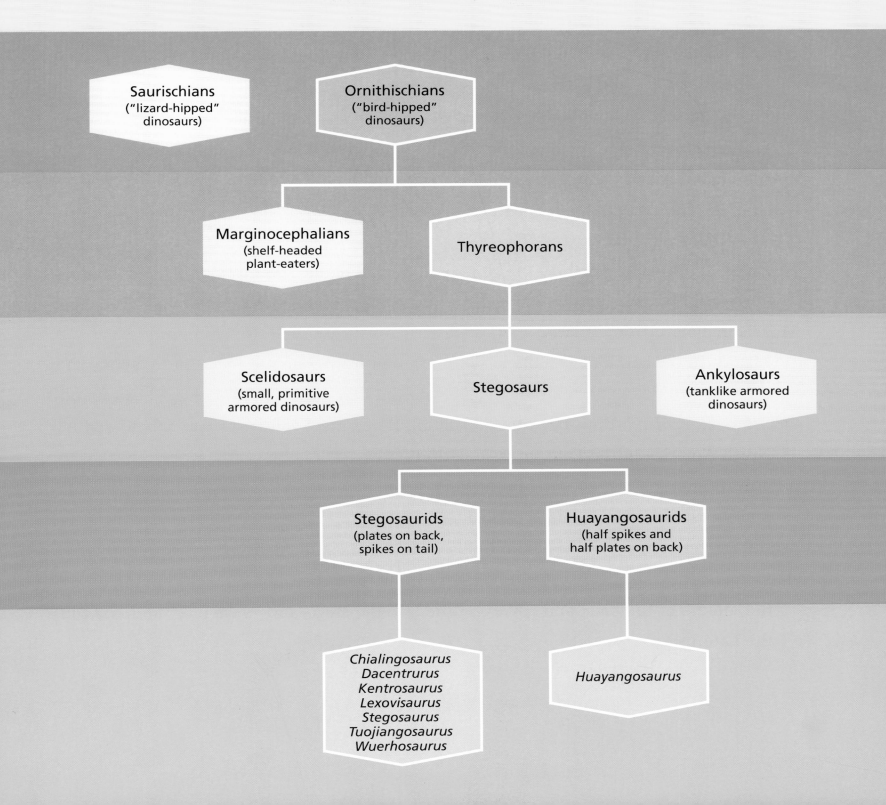

Glossary

Allosaurus (ah-luh-SORE-us): a large, fierce meat-eating dinosaur that was the most common predator of the Late Jurassic period

cycads (SIE-kuds): low-growing tropical plants with sharp palmlike leaves; their cones and seeds were food for *Stegosaurus* and some other plant-eating dinosaurs

extinct: no longer existing; an animal is extinct when every one of its kind has died

fossils: the hardened remains or traces of animals or plants that lived many thousands or millions of years ago

Jurassic (joo-RA-sick) **period:** the time period from about 205 million to 135 million years ago, when *Stegosaurus* and most of the other plate-backed dinosaurs lived

Morrison Formation: a large area in western North America stretching from New Mexico in the south to Canada in the north and from Idaho in the west to Nebraska in the east, where many dinosaur fossils from the Late Jurassic period have been found

Ornitholestes (or-nih-thuh-LESS-teez): a small, fierce meat-eating dinosaur that lived in North America in the Late Jurassic period

paleontologist (pay-lee-on-TAH-luh-jist): a scientist who studies fossils to learn about dinosaurs and other forms of prehistoric life

predator: an animal that hunts and kills other animals for food

stegosaurs: four-legged plant-eating dinosaurs with upright bony plates running down the middle of the back and spikes on the tail; the stegosaurs were most abundant in the Late Jurassic period

Find Out More

BOOKS

Amery, Heather. *Looking at Stegosaurus.* Milwaukee: Gareth Stevens, 1993.

Benton, Michael. *Awesome Dinosaurs: Armored Giants.* Brookfield, CT: Millbrook Press, 2001.

Cohen, Daniel. *Stegosaurus.* Mankato, MN: Capstone Press, 2001.

Dixon, Dougal. *Dougal Dixon's Amazing Dinosaurs: The Fiercest, the Tallest, the Toughest, the Smallest.* Honesdale, PA: Boyds Mills, 2000.

The Humongous Book of Dinosaurs. New York: Stewart, Tabori, and Chang, 1997.

Marshall, Chris, ed. *Dinosaurs of the World.* 11 vols. New York: Marshall Cavendish, 1999.

Parker, Steve. *The Age of the Dinosaurs.* Vol. 10, *Armored Dinosaurs.* Danbury, CT: Grolier, 2000.

Storrs, Glenn W. *Stegosaurus.* New York: Kingfisher, 1994.

ON-LINE SOURCES*

Canadian Museum of Nature Online at **http://www.nature.ca/notebooks**

The website of the Canadian Museum of Nature in Ottawa, Ontario, includes "notebook pages" with interesting facts about nearly 250 animal species. Click on "Prehistoric Life" for pages on *Kentrosaurus* as well as general subjects such as "Dinosaur Eggs" and "Dinosaur Extinction."

Dinosaurs! at **http://www.hcc.hawaii.edu/dinos/dinos.1.html**

Take a narrated tour of the Honolulu Community College's exhibits of dinosaur fossils discovered in Hawaii, which include a full-size skeleton of *Stegosaurus*.

Disappearance at **http://library.thinkquest.org/26615/index.htm**

Students in Singapore created this colorful website for the 1999 ThinkQuest Internet Challenge competition. The site focuses on endangered and extinct species and offers extensive information on seventy-six dinosaurs, including *Stegosaurus, Tuojiangosaurus,* and other stegosaurs.

Natural History Museum at **http://flood.nhm.ac.uk/cgi-bin/dino**

The Dino Directory at this website of London's Natural History Museum includes a brief introduction to dinosaurs and an alphabetical listing of species. Click on a name such as *Stegosaurus* or *Kentrosaurus* for a color illustration plus basic facts including size, distribution, and time period.

Website addresses sometimes change. For more on-line sources, check with the media specialist at your local library.

Index

Age of Dinosaurs, 10, 25
Allosaurus, 8, 18
Ankylosaurus, 25
Apatosaurus, 18

Camarasaurus, 18
Ceratosaurus, 18
Chialingosaurus, 20–21

Dacentrurus, 22

extinction, 25

fossils, 24, 25

Gondwanaland, 14

Huayangosaurus, 9, 10, 23

Jurassic period, 10, 14–15, 18, 25

Kentrosaurus, 9–11

Laurasia, 14

Lexovisaurus, 19

Mesozoic era. *See* Age of Dinosaurs
Morrison Formation, 15, 25

Ornitholestes, 18

paleontologists, 12, 20, 23–25

stegosaurs, 9–10, 24, 25
Stegosaurus
    family life, 23–24
    feeding, 15, 20
    self-defense, 8, 12, 22
    what it looked like, 9–10, 12–13
    when it lived, 10, 13, 25
    where it lived, 13, 15
    why it had plates, 12, 22

Tuojiangosaurus, 9, 16–17

Wuerhosaurus, 24

Virginia Schomp grew up in a quiet suburban town in northeastern New Jersey, where eight-ton duck-billed dinosaurs once roamed. In first grade she discovered that she loved books and writing, and in sixth grade she was named "class bookworm," because she always had her nose in a book. Today she is a freelance author who has written more than forty books for young readers on topics including careers, animals, ancient cultures, and modern history. Ms. Schomp lives in the Catskill Mountain region of New York with her husband, Richard, and their son, Chip.